Endless Journey

Sujata Mandal

AF520298

Clever Fox®
PUBLISHING

Chennai • Bangalore

CLEVER FOX PUBLISHING
Chennai, India

Published by CLEVER FOX PUBLISHING 2025

ISBN: 978-93-7500-838-5

DEDICATION

To the voice within—
the one I silenced,
the one I learned to hear again.

And to all who have ever felt too deeply—
this is for you.

ACKNOWLEDGEMENT

I extend my deepest gratitude to all those who have walked beside me—seen or unseen—through the journey that gave birth to these words. To those who listened in silence, offered comfort in chaos, and reminded me to breathe when the world felt too heavy—thank you.

My heartfelt appreciation goes to my family and friends, whose unwavering belief in me kept this collection alive. To the quiet moments, the unanswered questions, and the echoes of my own heart—thank you for teaching me that poetry begins where words often end.

PREFACE

This collection, *Endless Journey* was born from silence, reflection, and the stillness that speaks louder than sound. Each poem is a fragment of emotion—a conversation between the self and the soul.

These verses explore what it means to *feel deeply*—to hold within what cannot always be said aloud. Through longing, surrender, and rediscovery, they trace the journey of being human: fragile yet infinite.

May these words serve as a mirror to your own quiet spaces, reminding you that even in silence, you are never alone.

CONTENTS

Light Up My Core!

While I wait for others to close their eyes,
You sleep within my dreams on the starry nights.
One moment I cherish and long,
If only you knew what my heart wants!

Standing on the cliff I see,
There are not many but just one path
That leads to me;
Perhaps the only-because even if there are many,
But the chosen one is our destiny!

Many times I gaze up high,
And ask myself - 'only you - why?'
The silence then speaks to me,
'Isn't that obvious - I love thee'!

Be it dawn or dusk, or as the shooting star falls,
It's you everywhere, that's all!
Every path that leads to a goal,
You are the one to make me complete and whole!

Is it too much to ask for?
Wishing only you and nothing more;
A glance of you will just suffice.
Only you and nothing more,
Will light up my core!

Reminds Me of Someone.

In the core, still, I hear - the silence and more.
The loud and the faint beats, so near,
Are so rhythmic, without any fear
Reminds me of someone very close and dear!

But to remember, I never forgot, not once,
Then why do I think and say this way?;
I have just been in a light of hope,
For every breath I take, perhaps there is scope!

Wonder if, it is the same,
What I feel for you, do you too?
Even with my eyes closed, I see the rain,
For every drop, carries your name!

The world from space doesn't show the mad race,
For every heart carries this voice -
Just live your life to the fullest!
Not in any way - Just in peace and realise!

All that you hold, be simply bold!
There is nothing to hold,
Expect one- your name, in every breath I take
The life you give - do not break!

In the core, still, I hear - the silence and more.
The loud and the faint beats, so near,
Are so rhythmic, without any fear;
Reminds me of someone very close and dear!

Buried in Snow!

I don't know where it was hidden,
A treasure once forbidden.
For someone, it would mean the world
And for others, it would mean their life!

A ray of hope could hold it all,
At the right time would come and fall!
Won't it fulfil the desires of the heart?
As the world would see the rainbow!

Perhaps it's not that easy,
As you need to care;
With delicate love and
That's all fair!

The light of the sun would melt it away;
As all the treasure of this earth
Would bloom, play and wash away.
Those seeds of tomorrow are
Buried in snow!

Hold it Within!

In the stillness of this shore,
You can hear your breath
And say no more…
For what you see and
What you feel,
Is something far beyond
To the core!

In the boundless and
Endless sky what you see,
Ever did you feel-'That's just Me'?
So powerful it would be!
If only, you would stand by me
And see this existence through my eyes;
The world is beyond size.

So close your eyes, breathe;
Open your eyes and 'Let Go!'
All that holds you to
The limit and flow.
Take a step and walk
Towards that light
You hold it within!

Not A Crystal.

Not a crystal, though I wish it was,
To see what's stored inside,
To show, it's not as you think.

Not a road though, a path craved,
And walked by the journey
That leads to life.

Not a case, though I wish it was,
To hear what it said aloud,
To speak its feelings buried deep inside.

Not a sound, though I wish it was,
To ring and make the alarm that,
'It's the limit or it will break.'

Not just a brat, though I wish it was,
Made the music to thrive
With the rhythm to swag.

Though I wish it was not,
It's all that it is hidden,
'It's a mere - Heart'!

It Was Never Me!

It was never me,
At times it was you,
And sometimes it was 'they'.
At times it was time,
And sometimes it was numb.
At times it was chaos,
And sometimes it was atmos.

At times it was cold,
And sometimes a still mould.
At times it was said,
And many times it was unsaid.
At times it was quiet,
And many times it was might.

At times it was the rule
And many times it was a mule.
At times it was rough
And many times it was tough,
But it was never me!

Silence Prevails!

The voice that whispers in my ears,
Not sure if I want to hear;
It's vague but feels familiar,
Yet want to perhaps turn away
And not know in fear.

I know, it's perhaps once
Or maybe many times;
But then, it's not the same.
Yet, it's me the one,
It calls in the silence,
That holds the key of the time
And ages pass by.

Though the light remains the same,
Yet it is not defined.
When I choose to hear,
You are not here.
As I wanted you near,
There is much chaos in my heart;
Yet the silence prevails!

In My Heart.

Your silence is heard in my heart,
Though you may think, it's not.
For that you need to look into my eyes,
As not everything can't be told,
Held up in my soul, deep inside!

I wish I could show,
You were always mine
And I was yours-
The journey which is quite,
Hold my hand and we can
Just might!

For once in this life,
Make me yours and feel me;
Beating the rhythm of life
The song you sang
Is still heard in my heart!

Respect

<u>Is only then</u> -

When the lenses you have,
Set to see from,
Works exactly that way.

<u>Not mine</u> -

But yours, only when
I fit in that box,
Which you have created.

<u>Is predefined</u> -

By them and you and
Has to work
As you want to see.

<u>Drawn by the rules</u> -

Can't cross that line
Which is preset
In your mind.

<u>If boundaries crossed</u> -

Breaks it all and
Everything is gone
As I hold them none.

<u>My existence</u> -

Is questioned,
Not by you but by me
'Am I not enough?'

Lead by you -

Where am I? Why this chain?
My wishes? My freedom?
As just being human as you are.

Is earned -

When I will and only when I walk
By your rules and expectations
Well pre-defined.

Respect -

Me as me with my lens on
With my dignity held high
Without prejudices!

Look Into My Eyes!

In your eyes I see the world,
Held in times of infinity
Across time and space and beyond.

It speaks to me the tale of
Those unsaid and unseen journeys,
When you held me and told me
'Love you forever'.

I still see you have
That question in eternity.
When will I ever be there in these moments?

Remember I was, I am and
I will be there with you
In every breath that you take as I do.
Just look into my eyes!

As Simple.

In thoughts occupied about you in distance,
A picture is formed - just in my eyes
That I dreamt many times
May not be true as the illusion cast.

Held close to my heart
I can hear the humming
Faintly singing the lullaby
Putting me to sleep again.

As it takes me to those dreams,
I fear to see which may not be real
And broken so fragile,
Yet, I dare to dream again.

Hope, one day it might be the same
And true as simple as
'I love you'

A Gentle Kis

Peace and search doesn't go together that much.
I am checking on that life,
I felt I saw that right.
Not for you or for me;
It's just for those I felt
It might bring some hope
And mop away the blood
From every drop.

Search is on for you that is known,
Yet it is not there and seen unknown.
The paradox of life is so bright,
The light is seen, yet not defined.
Not any aspect that can suffice.
If you know, then may you show
Ever it could be found and
It will be so profound.

If it was so much then
It would give a hutch;
Mind and heart are not the same
As one drives here
And other drives there.
But at the end all it wants
Is peace that is like
A gentle KISS.

Blessings!

Held in hand, felt the touch over the head
In times of despair, eyes said it all
Yet unsaid and lips sealed!

Emotions tickled down,
At times in the gut,
Other times in the heart.

Preset sometimes by fate;
Sometimes man made.
Painful it is, but the might desire
To live breaks every rule
That holds it back.

Makes me wonder,
Is this all that we are made of
Or can we be just little better
Than now and forever?

The answer was 'Yes'-
Close your eyes, take few deep breaths
Deep and deeper- no thoughts-
You will surely hear that voice-

Faintly though, but will surely tell
'Be gentle, hold, feel and respect;
Care and just love'!
Feel that touch deep inside and
See the change!

Beauty that it hold
Will be revealed!
A blessing from heart
To you in disguise!!

Angels Around You.

In the midst of fog,
I sat on a log;
With my eyes closed,
In silence, I hear my breath
And the sound of the Universe!

Just been quite, just into nothingness,
In darkness, I see the light;
For so long into stillness,
I can hear the sound of life
And all that we hear everywhere!

But when the mind is still,
You will feel that moment of truth of life;
An unconditional love and laughter -
The laughter of life and
You see true angels around you!

Energy and Spirits.

Made of energy and spirit,
Crafted long before it's tale;
Never seen in the day
Nor at night, leaving no trail,
When you truly open your eyes,
Then it's form will truly prevail!

It's time to honor that nobody sees,
It's the guardian and spirit
All just in one;
I have seen it, so should have you,
If it rests in it's time
Then why don't you?

Never Give Up.

In the darkest nights,
Look up at the sky;
You will always find
a zillion stars guiding
You the way!

There is nothing to fear,
As the universe is there to hear;
I am not searching for hope,
Do you think I am discouraging
- Nope!

When I see the path so dark,
Can't take one step ahead;
But deep in the soul,
I believe and I have seen the whole
Universe guiding through the stars,
Saying to march!

Although I may fall,
But that will not mual;
As I tell you this, I gently feel the kiss
By someone I know
Are telling me they will show!

The path will be lit,
I will definitely meet;
So never give up as
In the darkest nights,
Look up at the sky!

Life Of A New!

Waiting in the scorching sun,
Looks like the golden ray,
Filling like the mist is the only thing
I feel, I get to hold you in my arms!

Crazy does that sound,
But difficult to pronounce,
The love I have for you,
Is the oasis that are few!

In the barren land of the desert,
Seems the art of the earth;
The ring that holds me tight,
Perhaps you didn't feel,
What it feels to be in a life of a new!

Times Flies By.

As time flies by,
The eyes see it all;
Many come and go
To the life that holds.
Captured in the lenses of the eyes,
Our soul knows it all!

The journey in the sky
Tells the tales,
Of all that exists in heaven and hell.
Few remains strong in the memory
And few just fade away!

Yet when we fly high,
The memories stay at the ground;
Where the world looks and says
'What goes around, comes around'!

In Silence.

In silence we speak,
Which is at times very meek;
Feeble is the life and
You are so far away that might
Bring the distance between us you feel!

But that's not the truth,
You will know one day;
Life is like a stack of hay,
Fallen down at times and flown away
At a far distance, hard to find back its way!

Not always you feel,
I will be here and sometimes there,
Perhaps everywhere.
Yet not for you that's always you told me
And I knew!

In my heart, I know you want me
So much and that's due.
For once, I will definitely be you
As you always knew deep in your heart
That I always have only loved you!

Experience.

From a distance it was destined,
To the unknown journey it was twined;
If only you knew, what would it be?
The perhaps you would say to me-
'There are times of every form,
Sometimes cold, sometimes warm,
Everything there it is now,
Always flows every time somehow!'

'Every mystery is solved by time,
At times long and small,
Just time to rhyme!' that's my answer to you-
Perhaps at times I have no clue!
Whatever it is out there,
It will happen and that's
How each life experience ripples
And turns out to be fair!

Then again it is not that simple as it sounds,
One has to climb high up and it hounds;
For the glory is not in its peace
But it lies with you if you can realize!
If it turns back to you and smiles,
You know you have conquered
All that went in time,
Will come back to you as a sweet wine!

Fly Anyways.

Far across the sky,
You always wished you would fly;
If not always but once every life
You wish this for sure,
And perhaps even more!

I saw that twinkle in your eyes,
Always said it's not a lie;
If I could, I surely would
Take a break in this journey!

Feel the light in that flight,
Where sun never sets;
I wish I met, but then I think
Life is like a blink!

Turn yester years
You have said goodbye to every fear,
Few though remains
But it has its own gains!

Not every path is a rain
You could argue
But again to have a good coffee
Don't you have to brew?

It's ok- don't think too much,
There are many puzzles as such,
You will discover one day,
You will fly anyways!

Your Eyes.

Your eyes said it all,
In your laughter it had the twinkle;
And asked 'Can we mingle?,
Not every time the answer is 'yes'!
But nevertheless ,
It's not always a guess!

As sometimes it can be in a real mess,
Perhaps, somewhere there is a base;
Though the lenses of your eyes,
You could capture every drop of that cry;
Which laid in rest and got dried,
And yet your eyes said it all!

Blown Away Card!

Hardly knew few,
What truly are you;
At least when you left,
You should have given some cue!

This was not just it,
I wished at least once we would meet;
Broken soul is hard,
Life fell like a 'blown away card'!

Never Be Me!

Years I sat with you
I was so sure and I knew
If ever you go,
I will be no more!

We did decide we will be together,
Now and forever;
Yet when the time came,
You decided all alone
To change the game on your own!

I know it was not right,
You had the toughest fight;
I tried holding you so strong,
Yet you with destiny played with me so wrong!

I feel your soul all around me,
Yet I am so scared and a lonely bee;
With you gone, it's not the same,
Everything seems to be a game!

Endless journey it will be,
Without you -
I will never be me!

Burning Coal!

You are in the plane where there is no end,
'Every form of cloud you see somewhere in the distance,
You will feel it's me.
Even if I am gone,
Remember the given hone,
It will remind you,
I am here, though you can't see!

All you need to do is,
Close your eyes and feel,
Even if I am in your thoughts
You will feel me that
You definitely got…'

For the times we spent all together,
The memories will remain forever,
'When the sky turns blue to red,
Remember me once you are fed;
Not the food that you know to cook,
But the memories which got me hooked!'

From dawn to dusk,
In every grain and husk;
My every form is now held by you!
My friends and you just knew,
I was scared so I didn't blew,
Every part of my soul is gone with you
And I became the burning coal!

Life As A Quarter.

When the night falls at the darkest,
And the stars are gazing at you;
Remember there is always a loved one,
Who is singing a lullaby too!

You can hear it in your soul,
Perhaps even your life purpose and goal;
Believe in the voice that you hear,
You will always find from a dear!

Whenever you feel like a fish
Without water,
Just remember
Life as a quarter!

Pebble!

Aiming towards the destination,
Does that really make sure,
The path of the journey one chooses to be in?
Not perhaps as you have been -
In the greed to be more happy,
We just make it more gappy!

It's not the word to reflect,
But I just want you to deflect;
No, you are not the balloon alone,
We all are blown gallon,
Doesn't make any sense though,
It's always about wanting more!

Forgetting the path we choose to be,
In the cry of 'WHY ME?'
Just relax for a while and
You can walk a mile
Look around you,
There are drops of dew!

Shining none less than the dazzling stars,
You too hold perhaps many scars!
Yet, you are beautiful within and I truly mean,
Make your journey memorable;
As your path will also be written
In every pebble!

Moments Count.

Restless though I am but you,
Only you can simply walk away in the distance
And watch through your lens!

I wonder many times,
If life is a big hive,
Every chamber has a story stored!

Not many get a chance to unfold,
That's why every moment
You need to hold!

Insecure it may sound,
Not really,
As life is profound!

Path may differ for many,
But the journey,
You can make it like honey!

Easier said than done,
But only you can and none,
Make every moment count!

Morning Dew!

Silence is whispered,
And whispers are heard loud in silence;
Not all, not every moment it is heard,
Yet it exists all the time!

Remember to hear your breath
Once in a while,
Reminding you, you might feel
Walking a never ending mile!

But it's not that bad as you think,
At times yester years just went like a blink.
Yet we do ponder around in the now,
To cross the bridges and paths as how?

All answers lie within you,
Always as fresh as a morning dew!

Makes it New.

Every meaning can't always be found,
Sometimes puzzles are all around;
At times just freshly picked from that ground,
Which makes your head turn around!

If I spell it right,
Then everything sounds very bright;
Trying enough without a fight
Perhaps I would put in place with all might!

Love that conquers all,
Never will make you fall;
You can be betrayed by some,
But never by self - not at all!

So believe in yourself with love,
Make your own tiny hub;
Where you can rely on your soul,
And truly complete yourself as a whole!

Drive the existence within you,
If you try, you will be among the few;
Every day the sun makes it new!

Memories Don't Fade.

Memories don't fade,
They remain as they were made;
If only you felt so,
Then you may conquer- go!

Life doesn't force anything,
We are just laid back, being;
If you think otherwise,
Perhaps the choices you make are wise!

Despite it's like heartbeat,
Yet we fail to greet.
Every path we crave,
At times it leads to grave!

Or at least we feel like that,
Sometimes slow and doormat.
Yet with every night comes the dawn
And with it comes following dusk!

When the journey is too long,
There is no point to mourn;
Inspired by the twinkling stars,
Shine from within near and far!

Highs And Lows.

One can say paths are predefined or destined,
This mystery gets solved as we unwind;
So many thoughts and feelings fused,
Leave us nothing, but confused!

Simplicity in the being,
Leaves nothing but the keen;
Embracing every choice we made,
Makes all our pains fade!

If we go as a reverse flow,
Life would shine and glow;
Let gentle breeze of love flow,
And settle all the highs and lows!

Sing And Greet!

Have you ever walked across the mountain paths?
They sing to you the song of life.
Next time you do, they will reveal the secrets you know.
Wonder- 'How?, this isn't it?',
Indeed it is, if you listen carefully!

As it is they who showed,
You different paths and made you learn,
To choose the right one;
Every time you learned the lessons,
You bloomed with a new mission!

If you know to pause and listen,
Every pebble and rock,
Every bird and hawk
Every bush and plants
Will tell you the story of life in every glance!

Voices you hear within,
Is the music of your soul;
Aligned with the path and the journey you choose
Every breath you take is part of it.
Just go out there and they will meet,
Give yourself a chance to sing and greet!

Race!

I know you were scared,
But trust me you are cared;
Don't let your fears rule the heart,
Test is just a part and it will depart!

This doesn't show you who truly you are,
This time is like a racing car;
It doesn't really stop
And you will take a big hop!

Let go of your fears my love,
And you will probably be flying like a beautiful dove.
Strength you carry with such grace,
You will definitely be the winner in this race!

In Disguise.

You wished I was a fool,
So you could think it's so cool;
As you would get what you want
And go on a rant!

But I got the wool,
And made a blanket into a pool;
Where I don't sink,
And take life with a wink!

Life is written in with a beautiful ink,
Blessed I am and the color is pink.
What you make out of it,
It's sheerly on your grit!

No one can argue it is brittle,
Then make a tea out of it in a kettle.
Look inside you, everyone is wise,
Soul is pure and the blessings
Are always in disguise!

I Love You!

Heart doesn't know where to go,
But it hooks to one it knows;
Perhaps it's not that strong,
But it is also not wrong!

Every bit is too long,
As you stay distance apart,
But you are still
There in my heart!

You don't feel that way,
I hope and think you may;
Just turn your back and see,
It's none other than me!

Everything said and done,
Yet there is none;
Only you who is there to rule my heart,
As you are my integral part

All you need to know,
I could never let you go;
For the only one for whom I feel,
Just letting you know, I love you!

Illusion.

There is always an illusion,
When reality becomes a fusion;
Of that which lies in your heart,
And then becomes a part
With the dreams and reality
Where there is no clarity!

In search of that perfect life,
Many a times we go through the knife;
Wounded and hurt,
grieving every night
And yet with faith comes the rise!

The feeling of being lost is there,
But deep down in your heart,
You know who really cares;
Pause is a must to grow,
Faith is much to have that more!

If only you knew, what I mean,
You would definitely be keen
To know what's stored more;
Still I will let you know,
The secret just lies within your core!

Life Journey.

I saw you in your pain,
How beautifully you hide it one grain;
Every step you took and gave me that look,
'It's just okay, I will survive!'
It gave me all the strength and the vibe!

How could you be so strong?
As if nothing at all seems wrong;
Though I can hardly imagine,
Just looks like a mark of a pin!

Life itself has been examined
And you carry so much discipline;
I did feel many times,
That I perhaps have many outclimbed!

But you stand me corrected,
Your strength was definitely underrated;
'May you be blessed with all
the happiness you please!'

'Let the divine grace unfreeze,
May the blessing flow
Like the gentle breeze
And the life journey be always at ease!'

No More.

Loss of the unknown when it makes you cry,
One may ask you, what's so special? and why?
How do you explain the connection of a soul,
Knowing and crying only for the loved or known
Is not at all a goal.

Life is beyond every explanation one can see,
At times we are touched beyond 'YOU' and 'ME';
There is actually nothing to hold,
Yet some souls feel like they are made of pure gold!

Perhaps that's what- you want to have,
And the tears fall as there is a big gap;
In wanting that treasure
Which brings peace to this soul,
From that unknown is no more!

Super Glue.

Every tiny step you took,
Laid the foundation and the hook
To anchor the life a little longer
And day by day it's growing stronger!

Walking and running,
Falling and crawling;
Like the ants, bugs and bees
Struggling and flying and
Sometimes just laying!

This is not it,
It's always about that Grit;
Of your hard work that leaves the mark,
Which speaks for you and
Your success sticks to you
Like the super glue!

Cheat.

Lucky are those who saw the birth so close,
The formation of life blooming and grooming,
The journey goes far and wide,
Some may not but others take pride!

The ultimate one is that
In all pains and games
When one finds a peace
That seems like a cheat!

By The Few.

The light that you see
In the sky so high,
Is the reflection of your soul
And that's where you go
As the ultimate goal!

Mysteries Beneath the Sea,
Are always so mystical yet meek;
Everyone wants to seek
And wish to have a crystal brick!

The clouds filled with rain droplets
And dew
The glow in the dark,
Is seen only by the few!

This Birth.

I was asked to seek
But I knew, it's not yet time
for the journey to start
Where you just want and you get!

Perhaps not very far,
I don't even have to drive the car;
Merely just because it sounds so good,
I don't have to get your food!

Sounds very selfish though,
As if ruined by a wild crow;
But this is how it works,
You and you alone got to do,
Or else life will one day smirk at you!

And you will definitely find it due,
To avenge on things and people you think
But this will bring you at the brink;
Unless you realize one day
All you have to do is, 'get up and get going'!

So here I am sitting still,
Churning every blink as a mill;
Embracing the heaven on the Earth
As all I have is just this birth!

Glory!

Shades of blue reflect the sky,
And shades of green bring the grin.
So fatal it is indeed
And it is not just a creed!

A mere dew and you can see through,
The entire journey of life it holds
As if you are holding the pots of gold!

Mind seems very crazy,
Easy to say and feel dizzy;
A chill breeze and you can really freeze,
Like all eyes and all these talks in disguise!

If you can understand, it's good for you
But there are always those few;
Who no matter what-
What they knew made you fly!

Destined in the eyes that line
Which wrote your story,
'Only once forever
You live in that Glory!'

THANK YOU